MY BEST POETRY BOOK

This morning my dad shouted

edited by Moira Andrew

Nelson

'For Katherine'

Thomas Nelson and Sons Ltd
Nelson House   Mayfield Road
Walton-on-Thames   Surrey
KT12 5PL   UK

51 York Place
Edinburgh
EH1 3JD   UK

Thomas Nelson (Hong Kong) Ltd
Toppan Building 10/F
22A Westlands Road
Quarry Bay   Hong Kong

Thomas Nelson Australia
102 Dodds Street
South Melbourne
Victoria 3205   Australia

Nelson Canada
1120 Birchmount Road
Scarborough   Ontario
M1K 5G4   Canada

Selection © Moira Andrew 1988
Illustrations © Macmillan Education Ltd 1988
This edition: illustrations © Thomas Nelson & Sons Ltd 1991

First published by Macmillan Education Ltd 1988
ISBN 0-333-46569-5

This edition published by Thomas Nelson and Sons Ltd 1991

ISBN 0-17-400677-2
NPN 9 8 7 6 5 4 3

Printed in Hong Kong

Acknowledgements

The editor and publishers wish to thank the following who have kindly given permission for the use of copyright material:

Bogle-L'Ouverture Publications Ltd. for 'Full Moon' from *Rain Falling, Sun Shining* by Odette Thomas; Jonathan Cape Ltd. for 'Magic' from *Where the Sidewalk Ends* by Shel Silverstein; Tony Charles for 'The Visitor'; Peter Comaish for 'Pie in the Sky'; Gavin Ewart for 'The Weather'; Faber and Faber Ltd. for 'Roger the Dog' from *What is the Truth?* by Ted Hughes; John Fairfax for 'It's Fishy'; John Foster for 'This morning my dad shouted' and 'Sand'. Copyright © 1988 John Foster; David Harmer for 'Dinosaur Stomp' and 'The Hedgehog'; Kenneth Koch for 'Weather' by Yetta Schmier; Judith Nicholls for 'Water's for...'; James MacGibbon for 'My Cats' from *The Collected Poems of Stevie Smith,* Penguin Modern Classics; Wes Magee for 'What is ... the Sun?' from *Calling, Calling,* Cambridge University Press; Gerda Mayer for 'Poor Mrs Prior'; Spike Milligan Productions Ltd. for 'A Baby Sardine' by Spike Milligan; Penguin Books Ltd. for 'A Dog's Life' from *Gargling with Jelly* by Brian Patten, Kestrel Books, 1985. Copyright © Brian Patten 1985; Marian Reiner on behalf of the author for 'Good Morning, Cat' from *Wide Awake and Other Poems* by Myra Cohn Livingston. Copyright © 1959 Myra Cohn Livingston; John Rice for 'A Mouse in the Kitchen' from *Rockets and Quasars.* Copyright © John Rice 1984; Eric Slayter for 'Sea Talk' and 'Holidays'; Vernon Scannell for 'Cat'; Edwin Thumboo for 'Throw the Ball' from *Child's Delight,* Federal Publications (S) Pte Ltd.

Every effort has been made to trace all the copyright holders but if any have been inadvertently overlooked the publishers will be pleased to make the necessary arrangement at the first opportunity.

Illustrations by: Ruth Benton pp 44/45; Val Biro pp 6/7, cover; Francis Blake pp 24/25; Kim Blundell pp 8/9; Helen Herbert pp 14/15, 36/37; Julie Hughes pp 38/39, 47; Sue Lisansky pp 18/19, 28/29; John Lobban pp 30/31, 48; Louise Martin pp 20/21; Ken Morton pp 12/13, 22/23; Pat Nessling pp 10/11; Maggie Read pp 34/35; Steve Smallman pp 16/17, 32/33, 40/41, 48; Joyce Smith pp 26/27, 47; Frances Thatcher pp 4/5, 42/43, 46.

Contents

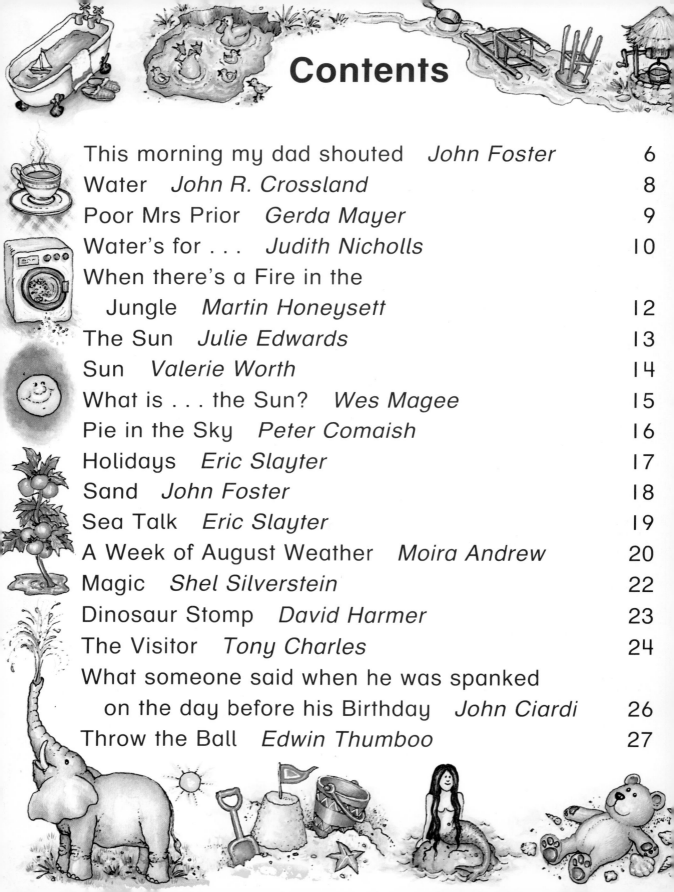

This morning my dad shouted

This morning my dad shouted.
This morning my dad swore.
There was water through the ceiling.
There was water on the floor.
There was water on the carpets.
There was water down the stairs.
The kitchen stools were floating
So were the dining chairs.

This morning I've been crying.
Dad made me so upset.
He shouted and he swore at me
Just 'cause things got so wet.
I only turned the tap on
To get myself a drink.
The trouble is I didn't see
The plug was in the sink.

by John Foster

Water

Water has no taste at all,
    Water has no smell;
Water's in the waterfall,
    In pump, and tap, and well.

Water's everywhere about;
    Water's in the rain,
In the bath, the pond, and out
    At sea it's there again.

Water comes into my eyes
    And down my cheeks in tears,
When Mother cries, 'Go back and try
    To wash behind those ears.'

by John R. Crossland

Poor Mrs Prior

Poor Mrs Prior.
Oh it was so tragical;
She went down in the magical
Washing machine.
She thought she'd come out cleaner,
And youthfuller and leaner,
Now nobody has seen her
Since Monday afternoon.

Poor Mrs Prior,
Oh how it must try her.
She won't be getting drier,
Wherever she may be.

by Gerda Mayer

Water's for . . .

Water's for . . . washing, drinking,
making tea,
cleaning the bath
or scrubbing me;
shining a car
or rinsing a shirt,
watering tomatoes,
shifting the dirt

. . . my Mum says.

But *I* say . . .   paddling in wellies
or just in feet
(puddles are good
but sea's a treat)
squirting at brothers,
splashing Dad,
soaking my sister
to make her mad!
Mixing with mud
to bake a pie,
spraying the dog
or catching a fly.
Bath or puddle,
sleet or rain,
let's all play
a WATER game!

by Judith Nicholls

When there's a Fire in the Jungle

When there's a fire in the jungle,
They call the Elephant Brigade,
Who race with their trunks full of water,
To the place that has to be sprayed.
But if the fire is a big one,
It happens as often as not,
That the elephants drink all the water,
To stop themselves getting too hot.

by Martin Honeysett

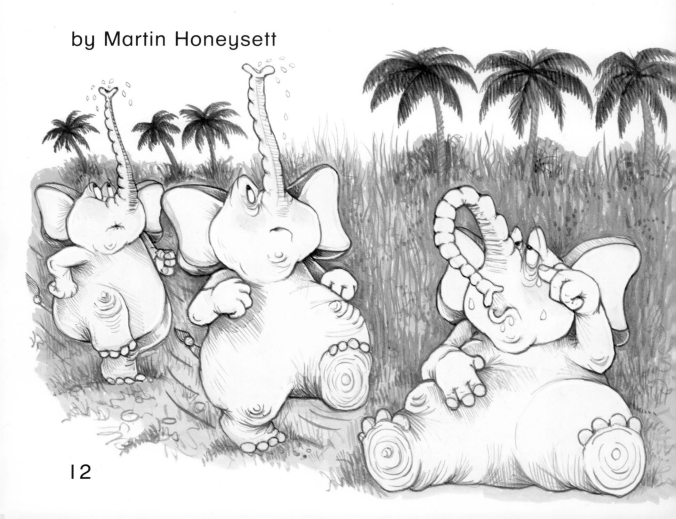

The Sun

The sun
Is round
Like a bun
And burning hot,
Hotter than any teapot:
It is a ball of flames.

by Julie Edwards

Sun

The Sun
Is a leaping fire
Too hot
To go near,

But it will still
Lie down
In warm yellow squares
On the floor

Like a fat
Quilt, where
The cat can curl
And purr.

by Valerie Worth

14

What is . . . the Sun?

The sun is an orange dinghy
    sailing across a calm sea.

It is a gold coin
    dropped down a drain in heaven.

It is a yellow beach ball
    kicked high into the summer sky.

It is a red thumb-print
    on a sheet of pale blue paper.

It is the gold top from a milk bottle
    floating on a puddle.

by Wes Magee

Pie in the Sky

Look in the sky,
there's an orange pie!

That's a lie, it's a ball
and it's going to fall!

Oh now don't look so glum,
it's a strange coloured plum.

But how can that be?
Tell me, where is the tree?

Perhaps it's a hole,
or a fresh bread roll?

No it isn't, you prune,
it's the moon!

by Peter Comaish

Holidays

Holidays are magic days
Different things to do
Different places
Different faces
Different weather too.
Golden days which quickly fly,
Till it's time to say good-bye.

by Eric Slayter

Sand

Sand in your fingernails
Sand between your toes
Sand in your earholes
Sand up your nose!

Sand in your sandwiches
Sand on your bananas
Sand in your bed at night
Sand in your pyjamas!

Sand in your sandals
Sand in your hair
Sand in your knickers
Sand everywhere!

by John Foster

18

Sea Talk

I'd like to meet a mermaid.
Yes, I really would.
We'd talk of ships and sea shells
And if she understood
She'd hold my hand quite gently
And whisper in my ear.
Though very, very softly,
In case the fish should hear.

by Eric Slayter

A Week of August Weather

One Saturday when the sun was hot,
We set off for the sea,
My dad, my mum, old Herbert Bear,
My bucket, my spade — and me.

On Sunday a chilly breeze sprang up
And the sea looked cold and grey.
To keep ourselves warm we tramped the hills —
We went for a *very* long way!

On Monday the rain poured down in sheets;
We went out and got terribly wet.
Then we stayed inside all afternoon
When books proved quite the best bet.

On Tuesday morning the sun peeped out
So we raced down to the sea —
By afternoon it was raining once more,
Back indoors again long before tea!

On Wednesday a soft sea-mist rolled in
Making the shore a mysterious place,
And I was glad to hug old Herbert Bear
With his tattered familiar face.

On Thursday lightning lit up the sky
And a storm laced the waves with foam,
So we dodged about from shop to shop
Buying presents for people at home.

Then Friday dawned a *beautiful* day
So we paddled and soaked up the sun.
We picnicked, built castles, found dozens
Of shells, squeezed in seven days' fun!

On Saturday the sun was still hot
When we waved good-bye to the sea,
My mum, my dad, old Herbert Bear,
My collection of shells — and me.

by Moira Andrew

Magic

Sandra's seen a leprechaun,
Eddie touched a troll,
Laurie danced with witches once,
Charlie found some goblin's gold.
Donald heard a mermaid sing,
Susy spied an elf,
But all the magic I have known
I've had to make myself.

by Shel Silverstein

Dinosaur Stomp

I thought I saw
a Dinosaur
buy a pair of slippers
in a big shoe-store
I asked him what
he bought them for
and he told me
his paw was sore
and what's more
began to roar
and showed me what
his teeth were for.

I ran like mad
across the floor
and bolted through
the shoe-store door
and nevermore
no nevermore
laughed out loud
at a Dinosaur.

by David Harmer

The Visitor

He said he'd come from Outer Space
just for a holiday.
He liked it in my bedroom,
so I told him he could stay.

I didn't tell my Mum and Dad
— you know what parents are:
they're always telling me I'm too
imaginative by far.

He stayed with me a fortnight,
and in that time he ate
space rations, my old comics
and my grotty cousin Kate.

He only meant to play with her:
he nipped her once or twice;
but when she smacked him on the nose,
he found she tasted nice.

I ran downstairs to tell my Mum,
who told me, 'Don't be daft!'
I ran outside to tell my Dad,
who laughed and laughed and laughed.

My visitor went home last week,
far out beyond the stars,
and he promised he'd call in again
next time he's passing Mars.

Now nobody believes about
my Outer-Spatial friend;
but no-one's heard from cousin Kate
since Oh-I-don't-know-when!

by Tony Charles

What someone said when he was spanked on the day before his Birthday

Some day
I may
Pack my bag and run away.
Some day
I may.
— But not today.

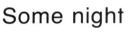

Some night
I might
Slip away in the moonlight.
I might.
Some night.
— But not tonight.

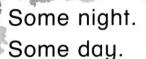

Some night.
Some day.
I might.
I may.
— But right now I think I'll stay.

John Ciardi

Throw the Ball

Let's throw the ball at the sun,
Make it laugh and sigh,
See it hide and smile and run,
Then fall from the evening sky.

Let's throw the ball at the moon,
And watch it falling down,
Then catch it with a silver spoon
In the middle of the town.

by Edwin Thumboo

Full Moon

Full moon is the nicest time for telling 'nancy story,
except the ones 'bout snake an' ghost because they
   are so scary.
Hide and seek is nice then too because it's light
   as day,
and Mamas don't say it's too late if we go out
   to play.

   Full moon to tell 'nancy story,
   Full moon to play hide and seek,
   Full moon to tell 'nancy story,
   Full moon to play hide and seek.

Arranged by Pam Frost

'nancy is short for Anancy, the Spider man, who is found in
many traditional African and Caribbean stories.

Full of the Moon

It's full of the moon
The dogs dance out
Through brush and bush and bramble.
They howl and yowl
And growl and prowl.
They amble ramble scramble.
They rush through brush.
They push through bush.
They yip and yap and hurr.
They lark around and bark around
With prickles in their fur.
They two-step in the meadow.
They polka on the lawn.
Tonight's the night
The dogs dance out
And chase their tails till dawn.

by Karla Kuskin

Roger the Dog

Asleep he wheezes at his ease.
He only wakes to scratch his fleas.

He hogs the fire, he bakes his head
As if it were a loaf of bread.

He's just a sack of snoring dog.
You can lug him like a log.

You can roll him with your foot,
He'll stay snoring where he's put.

I take him out for exercise,
He rolls in cowclap up to his eyes.

He will not race, he will not romp,
He saves his strength for gobble and chomp.

He'll work as hard as you could wish
Emptying his dinner dish,

Then flops flat, and digs down deep,
Like a miner, into sleep.

by Ted Hughes

A Dog's Life

Sigh, sob,
   gulp, bark, gush,
I'm soggy, swampy,
   saturated,
bathtime's something
   I've always hated!
I'm bedewed,
   bedabbled, water-logged,
my ears are frothy,
   my dose is clogged,
I might grow fungus!
   I might rust!
Bathing a dog
   is most unjust!

by Brian Patten

The Hedgehog

I've slept all winter
under this hedge.

Now I'm awake
I'll stretch out my prickles

stiff and sharp
like the rays of sunlight

that poke their spikes
into my eyes.

I'll snuffle and roll
along the hedge bottom

eating up worms
and fat crunchy beetles.

My first breakfast
after long months of sleep.

by David Harmer

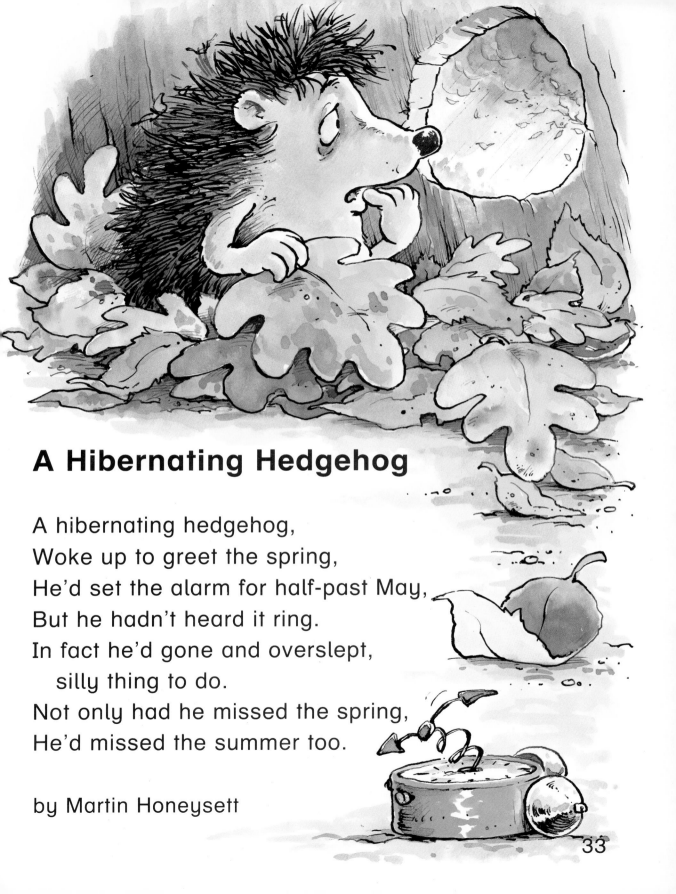

A Hibernating Hedgehog

A hibernating hedgehog,
Woke up to greet the spring,
He'd set the alarm for half-past May,
But he hadn't heard it ring.
In fact he'd gone and overslept,
   silly thing to do.
Not only had he missed the spring,
He'd missed the summer too.

by Martin Honeysett

Weather

It washes the floors off.
Then when it gets dry
You can sit in the park when the benches get dry
And you can walk on the street when it stops.

It's like a person who goes to do everything —
That's how the sky is.
The sky gets busy, she's working,
She's raining.
Then, when it stops raining, she doesn't do anything.
The sky is the sky,
And the sun comes out again.

by Yetta Schmier

Weather

Dot a dot dot dot a dot dot
Spotting the window pane.

Spack a spack speck flick a flack fleck
Freckling the window pane.

A spatter a scatter a wet cat clatter
A splatter a rumble outside.

Umbrella umbrella umbrella umbrella
Bumbershoot barrel of rain.

Slosh a galosh slosh a galosh
Slither and slather a glide.

A puddle a jump a puddle a jump
A puddle a jump puddle splosh.

A juddle a pump a luddle a dump
A pudmuddle jump in and slide!

by Eve Merriman

The Weather

What's the weather on about?
Why is the rain so down on us?
Why does the sun glare at us so?

Why does the hail dance so prettily?
Why is the snow such an overall?
Why is the wind such a tearaway?

Why is the mud so fond of our feet?
Why is the ice so keen to upset us?
Who does the weather think it is?

by Gavin Ewart

My Cats

(A witch speaks)

I like to toss him up and down
A heavy cat weighs half a crown
With a hey do diddle my cat Brown.

I like to pinch him on the sly
When nobody is passing by
With a hey do diddle my cat Fry.

I like to ruffle up his pride
And watch him skip and turn aside
With a hey do diddle my cat Hyde.

Hey Brown and Fry and Hyde my cats
That sit on tombstones for your mats.

by Stevie Smith

Cat

My cat has got no name,
We simply call him Cat;
He doesn't seem to blame
Anyone for that.

For he is not like us
Who often, I'm afraid,
Kick up quite a fuss
If *our* names are mislaid.

As if, without a name,
We'd be no longer there
But like a tiny flame
Vanish in bright air.

My pet, he doesn't care
About such things as that:
Black buzz and golden stare
Require no name but Cat.

by Vernon Scannell

Good Morning, Cat

Good morning, cat,
  you're in my yard
  and sniffing for a mouse;
  you might as well give up — because
  he's hiding in the house.

by Myra Cohn Livingston

A Mouse in the Kitchen

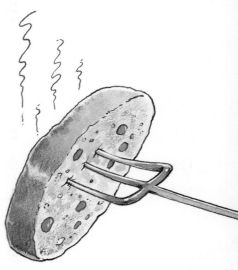

There's a mouse in the kitchen
    Playing skittles with the peas,
He's drinking mugs of coffee
    And eating last week's cheese.

There's a mouse in the kitchen
    We could catch him in a hat,
Otherwise he'll toast the teacakes
    And that's bound to annoy the cat.

There's a mouse in the kitchen
    Ignoring all our wishes,
He's eaten tomorrow's dinner
    But at least he's washed the dishes.

Note

Yes, I'm the mouse in the kitchen
    Thank you for the grub,
I feel quite full but thirsty now
    So I'm nipping down the pub.

by John Rice

41

Fish

Look at the fish!
Look at the fish!
Look at the fish that is blue and green!
Look at the fish that is tangerine!
Look at the fish that is gold and black
With monocled eye and a big humpback!
Look at the fish with a ring in its nose,
And a mouth he cannot open or close!
Look at the fish with lavender stripes
And long front teeth like organ pipes,
And fins that are finer than Irish lace.
Look at the funny grin on his face,
Look at him swimming all over the place!
Look at the fish!
Look at the fish!
Look at the fish
They're so *beautiful.*

by William Jay Smith

Sleepy Fish

Down in the sea where the fishes sleep
The water is wet
And the water is deep
And all the little fishes keep
Their eyes wide open while they sleep.

by Margaret Wise Brown

It's Fishy

In the pan delicious fish
Swim around a breadcrumb dish
Some like batter some like sauce
Some prefer Bird's Eye of course.

by John Fairfax

The Teeth of Sharks

The thing about a shark is — teeth,
One row above, one row beneath.

Now take a close look. Do you find
It has another row behind?

Still closer — here, I'll hold your hat;
Has it a third row behind that?

Now look in and . . . Look out! Oh my,
I'll *never* know now! Well, good-bye.

by John Ciardi

A Baby Sardine

A baby Sardine
Saw her first submarine:
She was scared and watched through
  a peephole.

'Oh, come, come, come,'
Said the Sardine's mum,
'It's only a tin full of people.'

by Spike Milligan

Index of First Lines